Strike Back

*How to Recognize a Spiritual Attack
and Turn It Back on the Enemy*

Michael Faherty

Published by Higher Site Group, Inc.

ISBN: 979-8-9951283-0-4

Dedication

This book is dedicated to anyone who has experienced a spiritual attack, felt overwhelmed by the situation and left unsure of what to do. This book was written for you. Those days are officially over.

Introduction

The concept of a spiritual attack is almost universally understood by believers, yet we often struggle to find the words to describe the pressure we are under. While every battle is unique, the symptoms of these seasons are remarkably consistent. You may feel disoriented, blindsided, angry, or hurt. You might even feel paralyzed or drained by the weight of the struggle.

While many books explore the broad theory of spiritual warfare, few provide a practical roadmap for what to do in the heat of a spiritual attack. The good news is that this book is designed to unwind the tentacles of the enemy and completely shift the tide in your favor. Just one of the truths contained in these pages has the power to set you totally free and overturn situations that have persisted for years. This is meant to be a resource you return to over and over; with each reading, you will discover a new angle of victory for your life.

While writing this book, my family and I came under a severe spiritual attack, the kind that leaves you completely blindsided and off-balance. We practiced the principles contained in the book and pushed back the enemy's advance. In the end, the enemy overplayed his hand. His attack backfired, exposing critical tools that were missing from the book's original manuscript.

Our struggle actually served as a catalyst, leading to the addition of a **bonus chapter** for your benefit. This book would not have been complete without the hard-won insights found in these added pages

Contents

CHAPTER 1

Spiritual Attacks Are Real

Ephesians 6:16 NIV reads: *"In addition to all this, take up the shield of faith, with which you can extinguish **all the flaming arrows of the evil one**."*

In epic war movies and period pieces, you'll often see scenes of archers shooting flaming arrows into the air at their enemies. The Bible says that the devil does the same thing. The devil shoots flaming arrows at you in the spirit. Sometimes, the things we are wrestling with are not just natural problems - they are what I would call a spiritual attack.

When under spiritual attack, some don't realize they're facing a demonic assignment from the enemy. Let's look at the job description of the devil. In First Peter 5:8, it says, *"Be alert and be sober-minded. **Your enemy**, the devil..."*

See how it says that: "your enemy." Did you know that you have an enemy? You might think, 'I'm just a peaceful Christian; I don't want trouble with anyone.' You may even be exceptionally kind, like my wife, who one cold February day, while sitting in the car, she noticed a tiny ladybug on her jacket. Instead of brushing it away, she took it off her coat and ran back into the house just to find a warm place for it to stay safe.

But the reality is, it does not matter how many insects you save or how peaceful you are, there is someone who hates you - and that someone is the devil and your enemy is throwing flaming arrows at you, whether you like it or not. It goes on to say, "*Your enemy, the devil, prowls around like a roaring lion looking for someone to devour.*" That someone is you. Sometimes these flaming arrows are launched at our lives without us even discerning where they are coming from, but the reality is clear: you are the target of the enemy's disdain.

And this spiritual attack can ravage your household. It can ravage your children. It can ravage your marriage. It can ravage you in so many ways. And just dealing with it in the natural doesn't make it go away. We must confront these battles in the spirit, staying mindful that the enemy is relentlessly launching flaming arrows at us.

Many Different Forms

This spiritual attack can take many forms. It might manifest as an unexpected financial squeeze - sudden pressure on your bank account that leaves you wondering where the money went. You feel the weight of that financial burden without knowing the source. Alternatively, you may find that people close to you - your friends, family, or fellow church members - suddenly turn against you for no apparent reason. It feels as though everyone is suddenly agitated and has a problem with you.

It could manifest as a health battle - a physical ailment that suddenly rises up, forcing you to confront a challenge in your own body and leaving you feeling overwhelmed.

It could be rebellion rearing up its head with your children. These wonderful children in your house suddenly act like demon-possessed monsters.

It could manifest as a major conflict with your spouse. Suddenly, tension grips your marriage, and before you know it, the 'D-word', divorce, is being thrown around. As a married Christian couple, that is a word that should be completely erased from your vocabulary. But when you are under spiritual attack, that becomes a valid option, exactly what the devil wanted you to do. He is taking shots at you with flaming arrows.

CHAPTER 2

The Objective Behind the Attack

Now, in each of these attacks, the devil has a targeted objective from the outset, and we need to discern it. When you face financial pressure and your resources are under attack, the devil's aim is to pressure you into withholding your tithes and offerings to your local church. That is the intended outcome of his strategy; if he succeeds, he effectively cuts off support for God's Kingdom while blocking the very steps meant to lead to financial blessing in your own life.

When everyone starts to turn on you and you're finding conflict with your church friends and family, you'll start to say, "Maybe I should leave my church. Maybe I don't belong here anymore." That's the devil's intent. That's his intended outcome for that spiritual attack.

When you get into a health battle, you say, "God is punishing me. I must have done something wrong." That's what the devil wants you to believe.

When rebellion begins to take root in your children, you might think, "Maybe I should just back off and let them do whatever they want to keep the peace." This is exactly what the devil wants you to do. His goal is to convince you to abandon your parental responsibility of teaching them the difference between right and wrong so that they eventually begin to follow him instead of God.

Or consider conflict with your spouse. You might find yourself thinking, 'You know what? Maybe we do need a divorce. We just aren't seeing eye to eye anymore, and things aren't getting any better'. This is the enemy's exact intent; it is precisely what he hopes to achieve through that spiritual attack.

Two Options, Both Are Wrong

When these challenges arise, most Christians tend to do one of two things. Often, they fail to discern that they are facing a spiritual attack and attempt to fix the problem using only natural means. Because they are trying to solve a spiritual issue with natural solutions, the situation never truly clears up. In fact, it often gets worse - dragging on for weeks, months, or even years - simply because they are fighting a spiritual battle with the wrong tools.

Or number two: they moan and complain that the devil is after them, falling right into a victim mentality, essentially laying down and submitting to his will. They adopt a "woe is me" attitude, crying, "Poor me, the devil is shooting me with flaming arrows," while they passively surrender. Both responses are incorrect.

CHAPTER 3

The Vision

One day, while driving my Calvary Blue Toyota Tacoma along the snowy backroads of New England, I was meditating on the scripture regarding the enemy's fiery arrows. Suddenly, in my mind's eye, I saw myself reach up and snatch one of those flaming arrows right out of the air. In one fluid motion, I threw the arrow up and twisted it around 180 degrees and as it fell back into my hand, I grabbed it tightly and violently thrust it into the devil's eye socket. There he stood, with a flaming arrow lodged deep in his skull.

Something leapt inside of me. This wasn't a passive scene; it was a violent revolt against being shot at by the enemy. I was going to make him pay. It all happened so fast, but I sensed the intensity of the Holy Spirit as the scene played repeatedly in my imagination.

The Impression Left by That Scene

The impression left in my spirit by that vision was one of righteous anger - a firm realization that God never intended for you to be pushed around by the devil. A graphic illustration of victim to victor; your transition from the tormented to the one who torments the enemy.

You need to make the enemy pay every time he takes a
shot at you. Make Hell regret that it ever sent an
assignment against you. You want demons fleeing back
to the pit, crying, 'Why did you send me to that
believer's house?'

The original working title of this book captured that
intensity: "Thrust a Flaming Arrow into the Devil's Eye
Socket."

CHAPTER 4

The Devil Should Know Your Name

In Acts 19:15, we read about a group of itinerant Jewish exorcists. They were not born again children of God, but they saw Paul casting out demons in Jesus' name and decided to try it themselves. They began saying, "I command you to come out by the Jesus whom Paul preaches."

The evil spirit within that man spoke up and replied, 'I know Jesus, and I know about Paul, but who are you?' Then, the man possessed by the spirit lunged at them and overpowered them, beating them so violently that they fled from the house naked and wounded.

Take note of this: the demons knew Paul's name. Do you want to know why? Because he was a devil-whooping Christian. When Paul and a demon had a standoff, the demon lost every time. And news gets around in the Kingdom of Darkness very quickly.

Does Hell know your name? It should. Every single person reading this book should have a name the demons know - one that makes them tremble and feel terrified.

Luke 8:28 says this, "*When he saw Jesus, he cried out, fell down before Him, and with a loud voice said, 'What have I to do with You, Jesus, Son of the Most High God? I beg You, do not torment me!'*" See, when a demon gets around someone who knows who they are in Christ, they fear greatly.

Big Devil, Little God

For much of the Church, the experience has been the exact opposite. They operate from a viewpoint of "big devil, little God." They essentially hold what I call "praise services" for the enemy. Every time you focus on what the devil is doing, you are giving him glory. You hear it all the time: "The devil's been after me. The devil's messing with my kids. The devil's got me sick. The devil did this and the devil did that.

And the devil is sitting there thinking, "I didn't even do half of those things, but I'll certainly take the credit." When you constantly talk like that, as a child of God who rules and reigns with Christ Jesus, you are handing him a level of influence and credit he simply does not deserve.

CHAPTER 5

The Devil's PR Firm

For many, the idea of walking in a mindset of mastery over the devil is a completely new concept. Here is why: we grew up in a culture where the horror film genre is incredibly popular. People seem to enjoy being frightened. Those movies - especially the ones dealing with the demonic -portray the devil as this imposing, unstoppable, and terrifying force.

In reality, that is just his public relations and marketing firm at work, trying to make him appear far more powerful than he actually is.

Over the years, many of us have been conditioned to live in constant fear of the devil. I remember when my brother and I were young, we shared a room and a bunk bed. One night, we watched The Exorcist on Boston's Channel 38. Even though they had edited out the profanity, the movie was still traumatizing.

I remember peering down from the safety of the top bunk and telling my brother, "If you stay down there, you'll be dead by morning. There's no surviving in the bottom bunk." He didn't hesitate; he scrambled up top immediately. My brother was so convinced Linda Blair was hiding under the bed that he refused to leave my top bunk for an entire year. That is the nature of a spirit of fear, and Hollywood has done an excellent job of reinforcing it. Conditioning people to live terrified of the devil, an enemy who has no right to hold them.

The image of God and the devil arm wrestling, face to face, locked in mortal combat for eternity is false. They are not equals. That image is a PR stunt. Satan is a speck, a single strand of dust, and God fills the entire universe and more with His overwhelming Presence.

We must renew our minds with the Word of God. For many, the idea that we can snatch the devil's flaming arrow out of the air, turn it around, and drive it into his eye socket is a radical new concept. But that is the reality. You need to keep that image in the forefront of your mind; you need a vision of victory because he is a defeated foe.

CHAPTER 6

Know Who You Are

So, how do we get there? How do we get into this mindset of being victorious over the enemy? Number one, you need to know who you are. You'll never get to this place if you don't know who you are and what you've become in Christ Jesus.

In 1 Corinthians 3:3, Paul rebukes the church, asking, "Are you not carnal, behaving like mere men?" The implication here is profound: you are not "mere men." You were mere men before you found Christ, but that is no longer the case. You are more than that now. His rebuke highlights that by walking in the flesh and being carnal, you are acting like ordinary humans, when in reality, your identity has been completely transformed.

Every single one of you - every grandparent, every woman, every man, teen, and young child - is far more than a mere human. In Christ Jesus, you have been transformed. The Bible declares that you have been born of the Spirit. When Jesus comes to dwell within you, you are "born again" (John 3:3-7).

As John 1:12 KJV says, "*But as many as received Him, to them gave He power to become the sons of God, even to them that believe on His name.*" You have literally become a child of the Most High God, vested with His authority.

God Inside Minded

The Holy Spirit of God has now come to live on the inside of your body. The Bible says, "*Ye are the temple of the Holy Spirit*" (1 Corinthians 6:19 KJV). The God of the universe lives in you.

Are you "God-inside" minded or "circumstance-outside" minded? You need to understand that the Greater One lives on the inside of you. "*Greater is He who is in me than he who is in the world*" (1 John 4:4). Know who you are.

The very idea that you do not fall over dead because of His holy Presence shows that He has "*made you the righteousness of God in Christ Jesus*". Jesus became your sin so that you could become God's righteousness (2 Corinthians 5:21) - the great exchange. This was necessary to become the temple or the house of God.

Resurrection Power

There is a scripture that declares that the same resurrection power that raised Christ Jesus from the dead dwells inside of you (Romans 8:11). Let's look at that resurrection power for a moment.

When Jesus was upon the cross, He took the weight of all mankind's sin upon Himself. He became sin so that you might become the righteousness of God (2 Corinthians 5:21). When a person dies as a sinner, they go to the place of sinners; they go to Hell. Jesus literally went to Hell in your place (Acts 2:27). The Bible says He tasted death for every man (Hebrews 2:9) - not just a physical death, but your spiritual punishment.

He descended into the lower parts of the Earth. He was there for three days and three nights, and in that time "He disarmed principalities and powers" (Colossians 2:15). He stripped the devil of his authority. He seized *"the keys of Hell and death"* (Revelation 1:18). Then, on the third day, He rose by the power of the Holy Spirit.

That resurrection power was so explosive that Matthew 27:52–53 records: "*The graves were opened; and many bodies of the saints who had fallen asleep were raised; and coming out of the graves after His resurrection, they went into the holy city and appeared to many*".

The resurrection was so powerful that even the bodies of those buried near Jesus were flooded with resurrection life and raised from the dead. You can almost imagine them stumbling back into town, saying, "I don't know exactly how I'm back. I saw a brilliant light, heard a thunderous noise, and now I'm here - and I'm hungry."

The Bible declares that this very same Spirit lives on the inside of you (Romans 8:11). That is the magnitude of the resurrection power you carry.

Jesus Body in the Earth

The Bible also declares this: "*Now ye are the body of Christ, and members in particular*" (1 Corinthians 12:27). You might be a hand, a foot, an eye, or even an internal organ, but you are a vital part of the actual body of Christ on the Earth.

The Scripture further explains that "*he that is joined unto the Lord is one spirit*" (1 Corinthians 6:17). Imagine I have two cups of water: the cup on my left represents God, and the cup on my right represents me. If I pour them into one cup and mix them together, you can no longer distinguish one from the other. They become one.

That is exactly what happens when you are joined in the spirit to the Lord. You become the body of Christ - a literal piece of His body. Jesus is the Head, and you are the body.
Do you realize the weight of that? You must know who you are.

Resurrection power lives on the inside of you. You are a child of God. And the God of the Universe lives and abides on the inside of you. You are an actual piece of the body of Jesus in the Earth.

Know this fact: The devil is a created being, and compared to God, he is a mere speck. They are not equals. He is not the "yin" to God's "yang." They aren't even in the same league.

The devil is a single hair on the back of a flea. Even smaller than that. If a mycoplasma, one of the smallest organisms ever discovered, could have a hair on its back, that would represent the devil compared to God.

You don't let this speck of a gnat oppress your life. You take his flaming arrow, turn it around, and drive it right back into his eye socket. Make him pay. You make him pay every single time he tries to mess with you.

Why? Because he is messing with a child of God, and the Greater One lives on the inside of you!

CHAPTER 7

Know Your Equipment

The Bible says that you have been equipped (Ephesians 1:3). You need to know your equipment. When you go to war in the U.S. military, they don't send you empty-handed; they give you night-vision goggles, a weapon, and ammunition. They provide everything you need for the fight. In the same way, God has not left you defenseless; He has given you the specific tools required for spiritual warfare.

As a Christian, you have been issued superior equipment. Luke 10:19 declares: "*Behold, I give unto you authority to tread on serpents and scorpions, and over all the power of the enemy: and nothing shall by any means hurt you.*" God has given you the legal authority to crush the enemy.

I want to expand on that for a moment. Again, the "big bad" devil portrayed by Hollywood is a lie. You need to view him from a biblical perspective. You have been given **authority** over all the **power** of the enemy, and nothing shall by any means hurt you.

Authority Trumps Power

Let me briefly explain power and authority: Authority always trumps power - and by a very wide margin.

Consider this example: On September 11th, nineteen terrorists used power to overtake four planes and crash them into the ground. On that same day, an official at the FAA issued a command: "Every flight is to come out of the sky now; all flights are grounded." With that one word of authority, approximately 4,000 planes came out of the sky and stayed down.

Authority is infinitely greater than power. Power was responsible for bringing down four planes, but authority brought down thousands.

In the same way, you have authority over the enemy. The enemy may bluster, and he may attempt to move against you with his power, but you carry the authority of the name of Jesus. Remember: serpents and scorpions are under your feet, and nothing shall by any means hurt you.

Paraphrasing Kenneth E. Hagin, he shared an account of his brother Dub's salvation that clearly demonstrates the believer's authority over the devil. He went on to say:

"This truth became very real to me many years ago as I was studying on the subject of spiritual authority. As light began to come, I started to grasp what had been given to us as believers. While I was praying for my older brother, who was not saved, something happened on the inside of me. It was as if the Lord stirred my spirit and prompted me with a challenge: "Why don't you take action yourself?" For years, I had been asking God to save him. He was considered the outlier in our family, and despite all my prayers, things only seemed to decline. I had prayed, fasted, and continually asked God to intervene, yet nothing appeared to change. But when that inner prompting came, and I realized the authority I had in Christ, I responded differently. I said, "In the Name of Jesus, I take authority over every work of the enemy in my brother's life. I declare him free, and I claim his salvation." I spoke it once with confidence. I did not repeat it over and over. I issued it as a command. After that, the enemy tried to plant doubt in my mind, suggesting that my brother would never come to salvation. Instead of entertaining those thoughts, I refused them completely. I even began to rejoice and laugh, saying, "It's already done. I know he will be saved." With that settled in my heart, I went on with peace and confidence. In less than two weeks, my brother gave his life to the Lord. God's Word truly produces results." [1]

Authority is Voice Activated

When Jesus dealt with a devil, He did not lay His hands on people to cast them out, He always spoke.
Jesus rebuked him, saying, *"Be quiet, and come out of him!"* (Mark 1:25)

"He cast the devils out with a word" (Matthew 8:16)
"Come out of the man, thou unclean spirit" (Mark 5:8 KJV)

Speak to the enemy with authority! An entire legion cannot stand before you. *"He who is in you is greater than he who is in the world"* (1 John 4:4)

Here are a few extra things you can say to twist that arrow once it is already in his skull, producing a little extra torment for him to remember you by.
"I cast you out to the dry places you foul beast!" (Matthew 12:43)
"I cast you back to Hell from whence you came!"
"I break the assignment against me and my family this day!"
"I command the torment meant for me to return back on your head, for the Bible says, 'the curse causeless shall not come'" (Proverbs 26:2).
"I cast you out, and I remind you of your permanent sentence in the Lake of Fire!"

Start all of these by saying "In the name of Jesus..."

Freely Give

Matthew 10:8 says, *"Heal the sick, cleanse the lepers, raise the dead, cast out demons. Freely you have received, freely give."* You are anointed and commissioned by God. This word is for all of us. You are a miracle going somewhere to happen. When you walk into a room, the miracle power of God enters with you. When you lay your hands on someone, you give God the opportunity to work His power through you. Jesus has given you this equipment freely; now, freely exercise it.

Take up the equipment God has given you and walk in your authority. You will never again walk like someone who is afraid of Hollywood's devil.

CHAPTER 8

Make Them Pay

Now let's make them pay! Let me tell you a story that leads into my last point.

When I was a teenager, I received Jesus Christ as my Lord and Savior and became a new creation in Him. I had lived eighteen years on this planet - eighteen happy-go-lucky years - without ever having a single negative spiritual experience. But within the first three weeks of being born again, while I was away at college as a freshman, I began to have demonic experiences in the middle of the night. I thought, "Wait a second. This has never happened to me in my life. I received Jesus, and now I'm being tormented by the enemy?

I realized this was not normal; it was a spiritual attack. I believe the devil was trying to intimidate me out of my new walk with Jesus, but the opposite happened. It made me run to my Bible. It made me run to prayer. It drove me to learn about my authority in Christ Jesus and drove me closer to God. I thought, "What a dummy." If he had just left me alone, maybe I would have remained a lukewarm, mediocre Christian. Instead, he pushed me right into the very version of a Christian, he did not want me to become.

Do the Opposite Times 10

Here is the thing: when you are under a spiritual attack, ask yourself, "What is the intent of this attack? Is it to break up my marriage? Is it to steal my money? Is it to get me out of church?" Figure out what that intent is, and then do the opposite times ten. Make the devil pay. Make him pay for ever having shot an arrow in your direction.

For example, if you feel the devil trying to keep you out of church, you need to adopt this attitude: "All right devil, you want me out of church? Number one, I'm going to start attending every service we have.

Number two, I heard there is early morning prayer on Tuesdays at 6:00 a.m., so I'll be there as well. I heard they have home groups starting; I'm going to join two of them and attend on both Tuesday and Friday nights. devil, I see what you're doing. I'm going to do the opposite times ten in Jesus' name." And if the enemy keeps pushing, let him know you're going to sign up for Bible school as well. Make him pay!

If the devil is trying to ruin your family or your marriage, identify his tactics and respond boldly: "You know what, devil? You stupid devil. I'm turning off my TV, I'm turning off my phone, and I'm going to read my Bible. In fact, I'm going to go through the entire Bible. I'm not going to watch adultery on my television anymore: it's done. devil, you've pushed me too far. I'm going to read my Bible all the way through; I might even read it twice this year, you bozo!"

Whatever the enemy targets, you must identify it and respond by doing the opposite and be strong about it. Have a holy anger rise up within you.

So, Mr. Devil, you're squeezing my money? Here is what I am going to do. I'm going to pray to God and sow a special seed. You were trying to get me to stop giving, so I'm going to give the biggest seed I've ever given, because I need the biggest financial miracle I've ever received. Go ahead, Dzevil, keep it up. I'll be the biggest giver in this church soon." Trust me, no devil wants you to give more to your church.

 If the devil is trying to lead you into hopelessness, depression, or suicide, you need to say: 'You know what, devil? I see where this is going. You're trying to knock me out because I have a plan and a purpose for my life. I have a reason for being here, and you're trying to get me to take myself out.

'Devil, just because you're trying to take me out, I'm going to be your biggest nightmare. I'm going to be the brightest light that has ever shone on this Earth; I'm going to be a spiritual lighthouse.' You know what? I'm going to tell everyone I know about Jesus. I'm going to start a home group and invite every neighbor I know. I'm going to invite all my co-workers, my family, and childhood friends I haven't talked to in twenty years.'

As a result, you're going to take the flaming arrows meant to harm you and drive them back into the devil's eye socket. You're going to make him pay, and he will be the one tormented by your resolve.

CHAPTER 9

The Believer's Secret Weapon

I have found that most believers are not prepared for a spiritual attack. It is vital to recognize when it is happening and resist the urge to fight this battle in the natural. How you respond will determine whether you will have a successful outcome.

When you are under spiritual attack, there is a distinct, paralyzing quality to the experience. The enemy's goal is to knock you off balance so that you shift from a position of strength into a posture of reaction. Once you are in "reaction mode," the devil can press buttons and trigger internal responses like fear, anger, and confusion until your head is spinning. In this reactive state, you are spiritually compromised and unable to make sound, God-led decisions.

When this occurs, you must recognize the moment and quickly deploy your secret weapon. Like a flash grenade detonating in the enemy's face, this weapon leaves him reeling. This weapon is: **Praise!**

2 Chronicles 20:21–23 KJV "And when he (Jehoshaphat) had consulted with the people, he appointed **singers** unto the LORD, and that **should**

praise the beauty of holiness, as they went out **before the army**, and to say, Praise the LORD; for his mercy endureth for ever. And **when they began to sing and to praise**, the LORD set ambushments against the children of Ammon, Moab, and mount Seir, which were come against Judah; and they were smitten. For the children of Ammon and Moab stood up against the inhabitants of mount Seir, utterly to slay and destroy them: and when they had made an end of the inhabitants of Seir, **every one helped to destroy another."**

Take note of verse 21: Jehoshaphat appointed singers to lead his army into battle. Their orders were to march at the very front, offering songs and praise to the Lord.

As a direct result of this unconventional military strategy, the enemy was thrown into total confusion, turning on one another until they were completely destroyed. Israel never had to lift a single natural weapon; the battle was won through the power of their praise.

Praise Confuses the Enemy

Praise is one of the most powerful weapons in your arsenal, yet it often feels like the hardest one to wield in the midst of a battle. How do you offer praise when the last thing you want to do is sing or rejoice? For most, the natural instinct is to shut out the light, curl into a ball under the covers, and sink into self-pity.

Let me be clear: that is the exact opposite of what you should be doing. True praise doesn't require a melody or a band. In the heat of your darkest battle, you can simply raise your hands, open your mouth, and release words of adoration. Bless the Lord and declare His majesty. If you want to get radical, add some movement—jump, dance, and rejoice for His awesome power. When you shift your focus from the attack to His greatness, the atmosphere has no choice but to change.

Understanding the sheer power of praise, I created a Spotify playlist filled with the most rejoicing and victory songs I knew, many of them from Israel Houghton's 'Decade' album. Whenever we encountered opposition and needed to stand firm in faith, I would hit play and begin to rejoice before the Lord. It was my way of stepping back, letting Him take up my battle and subdue the enemy on my behalf.

At the end of every year, Spotify sends out a "Wrapped" summary of your most-played music. When my 2024 wrap-up arrived, it revealed that the songs from my praise playlist were my most listened to tracks, by a landslide. Looking at those stats, I had to laugh; I clearly walked through some intense battles in 2024! But glory to God, He gave us the victory in every single one of them.

Casting Your Cares

Praise does something else: it physically shifts the burden from your shoulders to God's. By praising Him, you are saying, "Father, I refuse to focus on this attack right now. Instead, I am choosing to focus on You and cast all my cares into Your hands."

1 Peter 5:7 AMP tells us exactly how to do this: *"Casting all your cares [all your anxieties, all your worries, and all your concerns, once and for all] on Him, for He cares about you [with deepest affection, and watches over you very carefully]."*

Remember, when God has your cares, He is able to move on your behalf. As long as you are holding onto the worry, you are trying to handle it yourself—but when you release it through praise, He steps in to handle it for you.

My wife and I have praised God in the middle of so many impossible situations, and we've seen some of the quickest resolutions to our problems as a result. One time, we had a major need and brought it to the Lord. We started thanking and praising Him for the answer right there in our kitchen. While we were still praising Him, the phone rang. The person on the other end asked if we had a need and offered to take care of it for us! It happened that quickly—right while we were worshiping. It blew our minds. We looked at each other and realized we had stumbled onto a powerful secret weapon.

In our house, we have a saying: "We don't know HOW it's going to happen, but we know WHO is going to make it happen." God has a thousand different ways to bring about your deliverance, so the "how" is not important. When you stop worrying about the mechanics and start rejoicing in the "Who," you clear the way for Him to move.

Example Praise Statement

'God, I am thankful that You are God and worthy of all my praise! Your word says, no weapon formed against me shall prosper. I thank You that I have another chance to prove Your Word true. You are not a man, that You should lie. I rejoice in the victory that I have in Christ! I release this care and burden to You now. I put it in Your hands and give You praise that You are working on it on my behalf. '

Then take time to worship and praise His name. Do it until that burden lifts from off your shoulders and moves onto His. See it moving by faith. Do this as often as you need to. There is no such thing as too much praise. The enemy simply cannot remain in the presence of intense, heartfelt praise. It is a shield of faith, extinguishing all of his fiery arrows.

CHAPTER 10

The Devil Will Leave for a Season

When Jesus was tempted by the devil in Luke 4:13, it says, *"When the devil had ended all the temptation, he departed from Him for a season."* Now when you push back at the devil, the devil will say, "You know what? I am done getting my rear end kicked. I am leaving for a season."

That season might last 30, 60, or 90 days, but eventually, he will find a new recruit who doesn't know you - one who says, "Oh, send me!" This new demon will come and try to blow something up in your life and cause trouble, BUT you do the same exact thing: you take his flaming arrow, turn it around, and drive it right back into his head. You send another devil on the run.

After a few seasons like that, they start to run out of volunteers who are eager to get their butts whooped. That same devil who once left for only a small season will begin to leave for much longer seasons.

I've noticed this in my own life. If you are willing to fight back, those seasons of peace get longer and longer. Consider how demons acted in the presence of Jesus: they whimpered and screamed in terror. They are fearful beings. They may be sent against you, but they are terrified of the God who lives inside you.

When you fight back, they are not eager to return. If you are sick of the devil living in your house, messing with your children, or attacking your finances, you must fight back by doing the exact opposite of what his assignment had intended. He will leave you because he will not stick around a place where he is being tormented by a believer - a child of the living God.

Each of these principles in this book possess the power to drive every flaming arrow back into the enemy's eye socket. When combined together, they form an overwhelming counter-offensive that the devil is simply not prepared to withstand.

When Under Attack, Identify It

- Don't look to the natural to address a spiritual battle.
- Know who you are and let the righteous anger of God rise up in you.
- Use the authority you have and rebuke the devil's assignment.
- Take whatever was intended for your destruction and do the exact opposite - tenfold.
- Praise God right in the midst of the battle.

END

Prayer of Dedication

Let's pray together now. Pray this out loud and get it deep into your spirit:

"Father, in the name of Jesus, I understand who I am. I am more than a conqueror in Christ Jesus. This is not just a theory, but it is a biblical fact. I understand that there is a spiritual battle where the enemy shoots flaming arrows at me, but I will not be intimidated. You have made me an overcomer and have given me the weapons and equipment needed to be more than a conqueror.

Father, from this day forward, I draw a line in the sand and say, 'devil, no more!' I will never again be afraid of anything caused by you. Instead, I am going to cause torment in your kingdom. I will see the will of God done in my family and in my life in the mighty name of Jesus, Amen."

Salvation

You may have been given this book from a concerned friend or family member who recognized you were dealing with a spiritual attack. The most important strategy to defeat the devil is to receive the gift of God and become a child of God.

It is important to know that God is not mad at you! He isn't counting your sins and holding them against you. His desire is for a personal relationship with you. That desire is so great that He sent His only Son, Jesus, to shed His blood and die on the cross. When Jesus was raised from the dead, He broke the power of darkness forever. He did all of this so you could be set free from the bondage of sin and the fear of death, and step into the fullness of eternal life.

God is not concerned with the perfect phrasing of your words; He looks at the sincerity of your heart. He already knows you and loves you. If you are ready to receive Jesus as your Lord and Savior, you can pray the following prayer.

"Dear God, I have missed it many times and sinned, and I need forgiveness. I believe You sent Jesus to die on the cross for my sins, and on the third day He rose again for me. Dear Jesus, come into my heart. Be my Lord and Savior, I give you my life right now. God, thank you for saving me today, in Jesus' Name. Amen"

If you just prayed that prayer and would like guidance
on your next steps as a Christian, visit
MikeandLaurie.org and click the link on the
homepage that says, "I Received Jesus." There you will
find helpful resources to begin and strengthen your new
life in Christ.

Ministry Information

Michael Faherty is a Christian leader, Bible teacher, Executive Pastor, and entrepreneur based in Massachusetts. Michael and his wife, Laurie Faherty, serve as Executive Pastors at Living Word, a growing New England ministry committed to preaching the uncompromised Word of God with clarity, faith, and practical application for everyday life.

Michael and Laurie host a weekly Bible teaching livestream every Thursday at 7:00 p.m., along with a daily Christian radio broadcast reaching listeners across the Boston region. Their teaching is grounded in the authority of Scripture and emphasizes faith, and the work of the Holy Spirit. Their approach is direct, joyful, and practical, helping believers apply God's Word in real-world situations.

Website: MikeandLaurie.org
Facebook: MikeandLaurieFaherty
YouTube: @MikeandLaurie.org
Instagram: mikeandlaurieorg

Invitations

For ministry opportunities, speaking engagements, media appearances, or partnership inquiries, please email through the contact page at:

MikeandLaurie.org
or **contact@mikeandlaurie.org**

Works Cited

1.	Hagin, Kenneth E. The Authority of the Believer. Tulsa, OK: Faith Library Publications, 1967

www.ingramcontent.com/pod-product-compliance
Lightning Source LLC
Chambersburg PA
CBHW051337150726

47997CB00004B/1498